Soulless Heavens

To prevent wicked or malicious persons from doing you an injury – against whom it is of great power.

Dullix, ix, ux. Yea, you can't come over Pontio; Pontio is above Pilato. + + +

— From *Pow-Wows, or Long Lost Friend,*
by John George Hoffman

Soulless Heavens

The 2nd Collection
of Remedies, Maledictions and Directions

Jason O'Toole

Soulless Heavens
Copyright © 2019 Jason O'Toole
All rights reserved.

ISBN 978-1-7341254-0-5

Cover design by Kevin I. Slaughter.
Cover image (public domain) by William T. Horton.
Interior art by Jason O'Toole.
Biography portrait by Alec K. Redfearn.

The Red Salon
PO Box 354
West Union, WV 26456

In loving memory
of
James J. O'Connor
(1948—2019)

"Cattle die and kinsmen die,
thyself too soon must die,
but one thing never, I ween, will die;
fair fame of one who has earned."

—Stanza 75, *Hávamál*

Contents

Chapter 1 — To Make a Strong Key of Looking Glass to Open Enchanted Locks

1.	535/1	5
2.	Hallowed Out	6
3.	Rip Van Empty	7
4.	Emancipation Self	9
5.	SOS	11
6.	Needlepoint Roses	12
7.	Six Six Sigil	15
8.	Banks of the Americas	17
9.	All Flesh	20
10.	Impermanence	21
11.	The Cartomancer	23
12.	Lucky Hands	24
13.	Sunrise, State Hospital	26

Chapter 2 — A Failproof Charm to Still-Bind Thieves, Bad People & Mad Dogs

14.	535/2	31
15.	The Caretaker	32
16.	Dogwood	34
17.	Stitches	36
18.	My Jubilee Year	37
19.	Hematite & Quartz	38
20.	Jove's Oak	40
21.	Cinema Gertrude	44

22. La Lachuza	45
23. Red Dirt Deputy	47
24. Tramping Ground	49

Chapter 3 — To Compel Speech from Birds Nesting in a Tell-All Tree

25. 535/3	53
26. Black Seed	54
27. Elegy for Poppa Jack	56
28. Under the Weeping Willow	58
29. The Bargain	59
30. Accidentals & Escapees	61
31. Sky & Hell	63
32. Leaving My Senses	64
33. Nowhere Now Here	66
34. The Corn Pop Queen	68
35. Through the Bounty	70

Chapter 4 — To Staunch the Blood After a Fall from a Great Height in a Dream

36. 535/4	73
37 Child Labor	74
38. Public Morals	75
39. The Sinner & The Preacher	76
40. Real Estate	78
41. Airport	80
42. Hidden Panel	81
43. Soulless Heavens	82
44. Raido in Reverse	84
45. Stronghold	85

Chapter 5 — An Effective Charm to Remove Glum-Worm from Convent Schools, Ships upon Open Waters, & Solitary Places of Contemplation

46. 535/5	89
47. Conversion	90
48. Operation Wreck You	93
49. Godmonster	94
50. Saint Agnes School	95
51. Death Wish as a Prequel to Cinderella	97
52. Destroying the Animal	100
53. Charmless	102

Chapter 6 — A Talisman to Protect Against Elf-Shot, Witch-Stab, & All Paranormal Attack

54. 535/6	105
55. Bolt Failure	106
56. Community Corrections	109
57. God Is Very Angry	110
58. She Built a Bomb	112
59. Unwanted Apparatus	115

Chapter 7 — To Protect Parchment from Burns or Tears (Said to Be Infallible)

60. 535/7	119
61. Blood Castles	120

From My Dream Diary:

62. Board the Open-Air Sky Train	121
63. Broke into a Change Machine	122
64. A Family of Cabaret Singers	123
65. A Young Clerk	124
66. Returning Home	124

Outro

67. Samsara	126

Chapter 1

To Make a Strong Key
of Looking Glass
to Open Enchanted Locks

535/1

The words I'm trying
To say keep
Slipping down my throat

Hallowed-Out

To make man in His image
Blade thrust deep
      Cut away
      Our stem
Scoop out pulp
      & seeds

Hollow eyes, gap-toothed grin
Clumsily carved
Aping His divine countenance
Holding one terrible expression
      Against the night

The light inside
Is not our own

Rip Van Empty

Priest, what harm
To tell we ill-starred fae
    Yes
    You fair folk
    Will see the Kingdom
        Of Heaven

Do you also dream
Our skulls touching
Under darkened eaves
    Do you also dream

I couldn't be made to care
My sin, as you call it
Not choosing a side
Between your boss &
A regional vice president of
Lighting sales

    God, who cares

By the time I realized
    I never knew
What it meant to be
    Human

Was just me & the furniture

Now I sleep down by the quay
Until woken by a passing priest
Tripping over my tail

    Good priest, be kind!
    Tell me a lie
    Make me feel like a winner

Emancipation Self

Staring into your eye's reflection
Glimmer of malicious intent
Replacing bit by bit
That usual look of resignation
Above the marble basin
Where you shave & scry
Reacquaint with your likeness
Each day less aligned
With your self-perception

Nothing but those eyes
        Watching you
Through a concealment of lather
Applied with stiff boar bristles
Each pass with the blade
Reveals a stubborn patch
Of black stubble
(Your own beard is red?)
Fingers find your cheek smooth

& with your own eyes
Did you spy a fish
        A fish!
Along the bottom edge
Of soap & spittle flecked glass
A salmon pink with vigorous blood
Shimmering into focus
& out, it darts away

Your razor hand judders, you recoil
Slicing a red line into your throat
Above the sink
Your mocking image
    Unharmed

This is the morning
Always meant to come
No longer your slave
    The spell's power fades
Your unbound double
Trades razor for sword
From shuddering depths of the glass
The battle call of a war horn
    A clanging of armor

(First appeared in Wolff Poetry Literary Journal)

SOS

Hooked up to chest monitor & IV
Air conditioning on high
Freezing in shorts, no socks
Need a blanket
Have to pee

Dressed for outside heat
Socks in bin just out of reach
No one in sight
Men are loud
I cannot sleep

Near shift change room
Telling off-color stories
Don't want to hear their noise
Want a blanket
Can't hold my pee

Pushed call button
20 minutes ago
No one cares
No one came

Needlepoint Roses

The last of the rats scuff past
A fountain still shut off at winter's end
To their homes underground

      Rats fat on farmer's market vegetables
      & from the cafes
           Table scraps

Golden haired & plump Poles
Already at their jobs
Serving blintzes & pierogies
To ecstasy kids smeared in baby jane makeup
      Punks with arms full of dope
The counterman has an arm full of numbers
      Dachau tattoo

      Says "There's a fifteen-minute wait"

A boy in a disheveled wig tells a story
Of just how he got out of paying his fare

      "Did you wash your hands after?"
          "No?"

Opting instead for a bagel from the place
On the corner which is not the best
Ask the cashier why there are for sale
In his glass case
Examination gloves, surgical jelly,

Steel wool, & baking soda

    "People buy them"
    His sensible reply

March sun peeks through the gangways
Children comb the sidewalk cracks
Gathering empty vials & colorful caps
To sell back to the dealers, their brothers

    Not her again

She used to be pretty but that was last month
Abscesses, many mouths to feed
Undulate on exposed flesh

She doesn't recognize me
Grimaces when I announce

    "I do not come to slay unicorns
    In this weedy hortus conclusus
    Or pluck you
    From among a thousand sick flowers
    Drying on greying tendrils
    We call streets"

(Might have chosen words less chivalrously)

Her folk curse stuttered through
    Toothless maw
Fails to land

I haven't yet reached the curb
She is already boarding a station wagon
One like it will dump her cold body
Into the spikegrass, cattails & fleabane
        In the Salt marshes out on Long Island

This is not a love letter
        To a dead girl
Care of a fallen world
This is a loom knocked over by a drunk
See by the fuzzy warp threads on the underside
A city that was always a beast full of beasts

        & ever in the background
        Needlepoint roses
        Stitched deep in the tapestry
        Of another junk sick morning

(First Appeared in Nixes Mate Review, Spring 2019)

Six Six Sigil

You have built her up
Suffocating in the geometry
Of her shoulder blade

You have dreamt her up
No more than
A construct of your mind

Globes, stalks, digits
Encased in orange-peel skin
Airbrushed exteriors
Wet interiors

You are burning in

There was a time
When a beauty waited for you
In the forest clearing
With plaited hair &
Wind kissed cheeks
A home she would have made
For a man who stoked
Her hearth

You would not dare

You have charged the sigil
Of a corpse-goddess
Who turns your lungs

Into plastic bags
Full of tokens
For a rigged game
Making death last
A lifetime

Don't tell a soul

There are no souls to tell
She has used you up
Shutting down
Highways of flesh

Banks of the Americas
(After a Traditional Curse)

Oh Lord, master of earth
Avenge us on the ones
Who oppose us &
On the ones who have driven us
    From our places
& pay them back at once Lord
So that they may fall into hands
    Harsher than their own

Listen to me
You who oppose us
These words
    Are words of power

I bid you stand
I unlock the doors
Locked by your hand

You who have driven us
From our homes
Will find no peace
In your home

What profit a man
To gain the world
But lose his soul?
Lord condemn the soul
Of this man

That all he holds tight
Falls apart in his hands

You who have set us
      On the road
Will find all roads
Feeding upon your feet

You will wander off course
      No guiding star

Your compass points
      To avarice
In those bleak woods
You will meet yourself

The she-wolf
Has waited for you
      Always
& her jaws will have all the mercy
You have shown us

Any person, everyone
Who abjures bad things upon us
& all who call our name evil
& those who curse us
      All of them

Oh Lord you must bring them down from their heights
Just as all of them did unto us

Yea! At once!
      At once!
            At once!

    + + +

All Flesh

Three drops of blood
Stain a primrose glove
One from the mariner
Swallowed by the sea
One from the woodsman
Crushed under a tree

The third from the pimp
Trampled under whores' heels
& all of them you
Yet all are me

When the neck is ready
The guillotine appears
The wick never consumed
      Is never lit

Impermanence

Prince of this colony of dust
Prisoner of needle & spoon
His merry men won't take his calls
Biding alone in a rented room

Even lady moonlight
Has withdrawn her friendship
No airs from jade flute
Reach his longing ear

Cast off his moth-bitten suit
Stank of letdowns & smut
Rolled up his sleeve
Keen to rid himself of himself

Unwrapped the small square
Packet of crystal cold tinfoil
Tumbled out one of
His daughter's baby teeth

Came to rest in the crease
Of his ailing life line
In the palm of his left hand
Above the downward fork

Spreading halls of pain
Everlasting
Sprang from this incisor
All he has left of her

Perhaps there is some spell
To cast with tiny tooth
Purchased for a crisp dollar
Placed under her pillow

He can't even muster a wish
Carefully he places the tooth
Back into its foil packet &
Opens another

The Cartomancer

Fingers stained blue
Pry open the Devil's workshop
The tetched woman smiles
She plies a different trade these days

Her ruined temple
Scarred & pocked
Clavicle broken off
In rusted lock

Because men have needs
& women have needs
From lice bridled bed
To three card spread

You lean close to listen
Her words, a tower
Withstanding gale & wave
Lighting your way

There are lessons even here
Especially here
It is never too late
For one who still draws breath

Lucky Hands

Rubber boots stand empty
Outside the shower room
Plastic loofah floats in gray water
Scraped backs of sundry regulars

While mama-san snuck credit cards
From trouser pockets
& in the hour
Bought mopeds in Shanghai
Or bathing suits in Santa Barbara

Mama-san married a soldier
Boss paid him & he disappeared
Visa expired in 1989
Nobody checks, nobody cares

The girls catnap on shipping pallets
Four to a room in the back of the spa
Korean soaps on Chinese laptops
Antibiotics and Valtrex in amber plastic
Stand watch on a shelf

Kimchi ferments in a five-gallon bucket
Which props open the heavy back door
Leading to a litter strewn alley
Down which they don't dream
Of absconding

Laotian woman, Down Syndrome
Sold by parents at age six
Butterfly tattoo on meaty hip
To keep her from getting lost

Stuffing scum filled sheath
Into a Comet can
Replacing the lid
Hides her tips in a reproduction Ming
Imperial palace hastily painted in ochre

Tacked to the wall
Blue license from the Secretary of State
Issued to man she never met
She can give her name
Doesn't know her birthday

Going heavy with the eyeliner
The face in the round cosmetic mirror
No longer her own
They won't find her &
Anyway, they only see their fetish

Sunrise, State Hospital

Sun creeping over windowless husk
Abandoned police academy
In the parking lot orderly on break
Passes cigarette to girl visiting father
Committed to what we used to call
An asylum for the criminally insane

Stepping off elevator
Sting of bleach can't compete
With stench of urine
Flowing onto floors
Under ancient wheelchairs
As spasms slip twisted bodies
Out of adult diapers

Might pity this fellow
You didn't know his history
How lucky for him
How merciful
Mind shot out
No memory of profane deeds

Dried-out doughy arms
Sticking out hospital johnny
Splotched with tattoos
Bread mold blurry blue
Nebulous shapes of birds & crucifix

Playing Spades with the other offenders
In the day room
Unaware he's soaking himself
Still thinks he's getting out of here

Only get far as the solarium
Until death comes crawling along
Miles & miles of bathroom tiles
To put an end to this farce

Outside the orderly doesn't offer
To light cigarette for the girl
Standing gawkily
Sun in her eyes

Chapter 2

A Failproof Charm to Still-Bind Thieves, Bad People & Mad Dogs

535/2

Thoughts forming in my
Mind feel like
A spike through my head

The Caretaker

Off the state highway
In the southern part of the county
Along a hilltop, veiled in foliage
An abandoned dude ranch molders
Drive under rusted entrance gate that reads
      Bar H

Climb the narrow road in a low gear
Be careful not to fall into the dry swimming pool
Lying like a trap under a tangle of bramble
Sea of ungrazed grass thick with ticks
Tennis court shattered as if it fell
From a great height, trilliums
Unfurled condoms, & cigarette butts proliferate

The caretaker won't stop you from visiting
Not since that summer afternoon
He called his daughter home
      At long last
           Called her home

Estranged they'd been since
She married that loathsome boy
Who used up her best years
      Come now
          He whispered into the phone

He waited for the sound of tires on gravel
Crunching along the driveway

      Straight back to the house
           He kept alone

Fair hair had grayed
Since that day of her excommunication
Stepping out of her sedan
           Home at last

A single shot rang out
Embittered father punished
Errant daughter
One last time
Terrible & complete
Their reunion long awaited
By the bullet, terminated

Traveling from roof of mouth
Through skull's base
Tearing a smoldering hole
Into the pillow under broken head

On rare, smog free days
Standing in the paddock
One can make out the city's brilliant spires
Yellow roses peek through goldenrod & kudzu
Skeleton of draft mule bleaches in the sun

      There was a time it was lovely
      Families on holiday playing cowboy
      But time heals no wounds
      Wounds use time to fester

Dogwood

Is there singing
O'er yonder?
A choir singing
O'er yonder
Yes, there's singing
& someone's swinging
From a tree

On that coach bound for Hell
Thought I might rest a spell
Woe, but it wasn't meant to be
In a tavern like any other
Met a man, called me brother
Asked me would I like some company

Introduced me to his sister
Least he claimed she was his sister
Don't have to tell you mister
What she had in store for me

In a grove by the edge of town
Under the dogwood she lay me down
Spent my last silver piece & friend
She spent me

But when I woke sir, she wasn't breathing
Weren't my fault she must've been sickly
Purple marks upon her neck
Must've been some sweating disease

On a porch in an old oak chair
Didn't see the old crone setting there
Cast a binding spell from which I
Struggled but could not get free

Do you hear singing
O'er yonder?
A choir singing
O'er yonder
Yes there is a singing
& someone's swinging
From a tree

Stitches

In the ER for a couple stitches
Waiting an hour for anyone
        Anyone!
To acknowledge I'm here

Should have driven to St. E's
        This is bad
The knife just slipped
I didn't mean to
        Cut this deep

Perhaps I'll wander down
To the cafeteria
        Get myself a bite

My Jubilee Year

Against my temple
With rubber mallet struck
On the third
Joggled to consciousness
Am I denied paradise
You denied opportunity
To replace me in my holy office

Abnego!
       Abiuro!
              Abnuo!

Still it is my time
Yours could not come

Back from the merry Xmas
Of debt, well met
Not speaking mere ex cathedra
Recognize not oraculum?
Every love-wrought word a jewel!
Jewels circling a diadem
Never to prettify
Your mendacious head

For you I have fashioned
This garland of plastic lilies
Which blew over
       The cemetery fence
It will please me if you wear it
If you must be
       In my presence

Hematite & Quartz

Filled my pockets
With hematite & quartz
Made the sign of the cross
Prayed nine novenas
Lit a candle ringed with salt

Have oil blessed
By Padre Pio
Washed in the water of Lourdes
A splinter of the True Cross
Cloth touched to a relic of
Saint Sebastian

But they can't protect me from you
They're no damn good
Against you

Devil's shoestring &
Johnny Conqueroo
In a red flannel bag
A splinter of the True Crib
Relic of Saint
Who-damn-cares?

Been no help against you
Can't protect me from…
You say you're from heaven
You're the reason I'm going to
       Hell

Got mojo beans &
Dragon's blood
Scrubbed my floors with
Florida Water
You broke my conjure hand
Showed me signs & wonders in
Your wicked parlor

Snuffed my white candle
Set alight the red
Can't protect me from you
Nothing keeps me from…

Jove's Oak

The unchurched
You called us
We made our shrine
Under the wizened branches
Of an ancient oak

We'd settle our disputes
Square our deals
Bless unions

Or dissolve them

You whispered how we
Hung thieves from her boughs
Even chittered about
Sacrificial rites under that tree
To remove the ringspot
Cursing our tomatoes

We might have

& black incantations
Weird divinations
Nubile womenfolk clad only
In coronets of white carnations!

It's true Pawpaw
Employed a forked branch
Dropped from our oak

To show where to dig our well
& we may have had a conjure woman

We may still

Mothers seen their young'uns off
With green cuttings
In their lapel buttons
Gamblers
Heading for the tables upstate
A piece of root
In their mojo bags

But weren't no devilry

A Sunday like any other
We woke to a choir of
Pinch-faced women
Sacred harp singing
A sound far sweeter
Than their disagreeable features
Might suggest

But who is this man

Under the tree
Flanked by two deputies
Young preaching man
Stripped nekkid to the waist
Chalk white skin
Scrubbed cheeks

Barely sprouting whiskers

Over his shoulder
Shiny axe
Straight from the hardware store
Not even applied to a whetstone

Too dull to cut cultured butter

Shouted an invocation
To the Holy Spirit
That his God would defeat our imps
& strike down this demon tree
With roots gone down to Hell

His people raised a whoop

When his limp swing
Connected with the outer-bark
He took another hack or two
Making no dint whatsoever

Axe fell from soft hands

A team stepped forward
& set to work felling that oak
A wail rose up from our women
Mema slapped that preacher
Across his ruddy face
& was pulled off

By a bored deputy

Until late in the afternoon they worked
A groaning, eldritch voice
Emanating from the innermost rings
Woken by the misery whip's fatal motion
Vexed our mortal souls
In a forgotten tongue &
With a great creak
Toppled over crashing
To the ground

Preacher claimed he alone

With a little help from his God
Felled that heathen tree
With one blow from his consecrated axe
Blessed in his buck a bottle holy water

Same as he sold the rubes in town

With lumber from that strong oak
They built their church
In the mountain-hollow
Where the whims of the elements
Are anyone's guess
Never know when or where
Lightning might strike
That tree stood for six hundred years

Their church, not even one

Cinema Gertrude

Behind the glass booth the woman
Sat smiling
        Rats swarming around her
        Big rats, little rats

A display advertisement for the new film
Your date is forcing you to see
        The woman & the rats
Feign a smile to cover up your disgust

Everyone does the same

        Rats like regrets run frenzied
Trapped behind the glass with the woman
        Rats making you ill with cruel logic
Damn it! You say as you search for a rock
Finding nothing to shatter this glass

Exit the theater mourning your lost evening
        Rats lie at the bottom of the display
Bent spines & twisted necks
        Some with tails chewed off

No apology will be forthcoming
No refunds
The woman sat smiling

La Lachuza (The Owl Woman)

The brujo wants two grand
To remove the curse her
Brother's common law paid
To hex her house & home
No curse! It's heroin

You see things, act loco
That spray paint you all huff
From Big Red cans leaving
Gold circles on your mouths
No sir! Come back tonight

You'll see *La Lachuza's*
Eyes glow red in the trees
Red eyes? You mean tail lights
See the Silverado
In the driveway kitty

Corner to where we stand?
No sir! We must pay him
We must pay the brujo
To lift this evil curse
Do you believe in Him?

Pointing at the wall sized
Painting of the Sermon
On the Mount, wormwood frame
Hung lopsided above
Stolen television

El Señor! Yes of course
We do love El Señor!
He does so many tricks
But the brujo has more
Powerful black magic

Red Dirt Deputy

Still talking when we got there
Hit that Georgia pine
      Doing eighty
No airbag or seatbelt
Somehow still alive
Whispered he bonded out of county

Just in time for Christmas
Went home found her gone
Note on the fridge said he
Best be departed
By the time she returned

Engine 2 boys pried open
Road physics crushed cab
Boozy life spilled onto floorboards
Red-coating Natty Ice empties
Dash pinning him to bucket seat
Was all that held him together

Grabbed a bologna on white
& a Tab from the ER fridge
Stood over him on the slab
Pressed into his abdomen
With my non-sandwich hand

His torso rippled
For a full minute
No intact rib bones

To halt the ebb & flow

Searching for his home
Turned off the main road
Into a low rent subdivision
Figured I'd find mama
Expanding into her rocker recliner
Plastic forking pulled pork
From a Styrofoam container
The races on a Rent-A-Center TV

But the road narrowed
Down long, hidden drive
Through allée of imposing elms
Opened into an antebellum scene
Coppery sunset dripped down
Doric columns forever loitering
As I approached the front portico
Bearing gravest news

Door chime echoed in the center hall
        No answer from within

In the hothouse
Found the caretaker
Devotedly tending the inner-garden
Inquired as to whereabouts
Lady of the manor

"She's wintering in Monaco"

Tramping Ground

I've been running & hiding
& thieving & lying
Been shooting, stabbing
Killing ain't nothing
Been thirsting, starving
Feeding on the shadows
Racing & chasing
The serpent in your garden

Blood stains the front of my work shirt
Because the work that I do
Is the filthy, grunt work
Of the gentleman with the pitchfork
Scratch found work for
These slack hands
Killing work for
Blood-black hands

I've been chanting & praying
To the weird thing in the corner
Been driving flat out
To outrun my terror

Why
Do birds fall from the sky
Every time
I walk by?

Scarlet smiles on snow white throats
Rope burns on thin white wrists
I am the one that hurts
I am the one called "Hurt"

Round & round
This mortal coil
Round & round
This infertile soil
Round & round
The serpent's tail
Round & round
My tramping ground

Chapter 3

To Compel Speech
from Birds
Nesting in a Tell-All Tree

535/3

Halogens reveal
Silver fox
Almost out of luck

Black Seed

I set out a bird feeder
At the winter solstice
No birds came
Millet & thistle seed
  Rotted black

I hung a cake of suet
Powerful fuel for cardinal & finch
To survive the harshest months
There it remained
  Untouched

I could hear them singing
In my neighbors' trees
Titmice & jays
Would not show themselves to me

Perhaps bread crumbs will entice them

In the morning, paw prints in the snow
Showed the path of some mammal
Came at night to claim these morsels
  Of stale hotdog buns

Didn't recognize those prints
That set out from the dumpster
Returning there for curried chicken bones
  & yogurt cups

They have strange animals here
Maybe those aren't birds at all
Maybe I am only imagining
That I can hear their song

Elegy for Poppa Jack

Rip out that catheter
Shake off that hospital gown
& Demerol sleep
There's a game on the television
& a roast beef on rye with your name on it

Wipe off that makeup
& punch out the funeral director
Kick over the coffin
& drive your Cadillac into
The Northshore night
There's still time
To walk along the Sound
Watching the lights
Of Connecticut

Don't let them carry you
Out of Saint Pat's like some
Comatose drunk
Joke about Father's firm handshake
& brotherly love forgotten
In the race out of the parking lot

Miss that flight to Saint Louis
It leaves your sons behind
Rise from your cigar ashes
Let me see you standing
Man that you are

For this last memory of you
Unconscious in a hospital bed
With that catheter
That's not the man I knew

Instead, drive us out to Jones Beach
Where the waves knock me down
Fear overtakes me
I can't escape the undertow
You pull me free
& stand me upright
You don't let me die

How I tried to do the same for you
Now I must let you go

(First appeared in An Anthology of Poems from The Red Salon, 2018)

Under the Weeping Willow

Oftentimes, inchworms
Would tumble from the weeping willow
Onto our heads
Into our drinks

We would rescue them
Gently set them free on the lawn
Dropped from our fingers
On invisible threads

Grandfather didn't get to spend his last days
In the shade of the willow's low branches
Smoking his cigars at the cast iron table
Painted white

He died an American death
In an antiseptic cancer ward
On the third floor, a parking lot view
Head shaved, sliced open
Beyond the surgeon's skill

I know I will always find him
When I close my eyes
Cigar in hand
Under his weeping willow
In his inchworm empire

(First appeared in We've Seen the Same Horizon, 2019)

The Bargain

Glower at the day's news
Conjured with forefinger
On my radiant tablet

In the past
I too, did violence
On behalf of innocence
There were monsters in those days
For fourteen dollars an hour
I beat them back

Today I have chosen differently
I've made & drank
A cup of tea

Made a pact with a stray cat
The field mice are yours
But please striped & gray cat
Leave be the singing birds
    "What singing birds?"
Crooned the cat

With the clouds overhead
I struck a bargain
Let's have that storm, clouds gray & pregnant
Now, while I am yet at home
Sipping tea
    "Yes, or possibly later
    While you are driving narrow roads

  Over the dark hills"
Shrugged the clouds

I stood barefoot in the mud
Called to death as a friend
Deliver my flesh to the earth on which I stand
Just grant that my good name lives on
  "Why would I grant a friend so dear
  A favor so worthless?"
Asked death, who answered
  "My wish is that you understand
  That you freely give your life to me"

& so, I made another cup of tea
As the cat, goldfinch in his jaws
Slunk into the bushes
To escape the driving rain

Accidentals & Escapees

Manhattan spring stroll
Led me past a park bench
Sat there an old woman
Gone blue with death
Green parakeet alighted
Onto her shoulder drooped & stiff
Pecked a hole into her cheek
Right outside Bellevue
We pretended not to see
How could we?

Outside the auto dealership
Selling me a kid hauler
For my Irish twins
Blue parakeet fluttering
Tittering & delighting my babies
Until it flew off & shot
Across I-20
Smacked by the drop visor
Of a speeding Peterbilt

Was that a god damned dinosaur?
The impossible raptor
Standing grade-schooler high
Along I-35
Just above Laredo
Motorcycle jacket wings
Wide as my bumper
Horrible beak long & sloping

Elongated neck ringed red, white & black
Not in my Peterson's Guide
Ornithologist wrote back
I wasn't the only one who saw
This thing that shouldn't be

Sky & Hell

Seen from attic window
Bowl of twig & twine
Topping leafless oak

Bandolier of wrung-necked
Mourning doves
Lining nest
Orderly in death

Eagle returning
From exploits & entanglements
Frail dawn rays
Drain through buckshot pierced
Void-black feathers

Shattered wing raised
To all above
Sinister, lowered
To a society of lice & mites
Officiously devouring
Lifeless doves

Leaving My Senses

Cold & alone
Thrown from my home
I will find trouble
Wherever I roam

Every time I'm
At the top of my game
I drink my way down
To the bottom again

Rolling in late
With bloodshot eyes
The wife throws me out
What a god damn surprise

Back out I go
To the nudie bar
For a table dance
& a cold PBR

I'd stay forever
But I'm out on my ass
When a girl with fake breasts
Gets the last of my cash

Oversleep
Miss my train
Guess I'll be looking
For a job again

On Judgment Day
There'll be hell to pay
For the shots, the pints
& the whores

In my coffin
Dead as a nail I'll lay
Children will say
We don't know you
Old man

I'm leaving my senses

Nowhere Now Here

We have traced our dying roots back to you
From beyond the suffocating confines
Of your verdant lore
    We are virus
    In angelic hosts

Lift up your hearts!
Or if you please, talismans
& armaments
    Still we come

We are all your Captain Cooks come at once
With your nose pressed to our deck
Will you see our terrible ship?
    It stands in the poisoned lagoon,
In the lifeless forest clearing &
Your carport
    Where your fattened children play

Will you believe in the fullness of providence?
When at last we touch
Across sullied worlds, from bleak firmaments
To trembling earths
    Will you believe?

Thrones, many-eyed wheels
Turn in that space
Between thought &
    Form

They sing, but not for glory:

"Each season brings a shocking new turn
You long for the flame that no longer burns
Something crunches underfoot
Your children's blackened bones"

>Snap dry, stinking fruit off branches
>Wrest promises off spiny stalks
>Cutting palms, stigmata of the unfaithful
>Feed the mouth that cries
>With balled up fist!

"In shame you turn away from our face
Dying won't carry you off from this place
Avengers shall not pass over your homes
Foundations laid with your children's bones"

>Reaching for answers we can't understand
>Grasping for branches that slice up our hands
>Through spray of blood & broken tooth
>>Thank you for this harvest!

The Corn Pop Queen

How could we as children know
Why a clown leered, dementedly
From our box of frosted wheat
Our toasted oats or puffed rice
Or crunchy sweetened corn pops
Fortifying us with iron
We little men of iron
Princes of the breakfast nook

At the last circuses there were clowns
But they neglected their godly function
Ringmasters no longer released
Foxes with tails aflame
To cleanse the crops
We who bless our fields with Bayer Requiem
Have no need for some goddess
Whose name we've forgotten
Though it's printed right on the box

No pregnant sow offered
To the Corn Pop Queen
Who has time for bacon
In morning's frenzied rush?
No bawdy crone to lift her skirt
A plate of pork
A gift of mirth

As mother frets for a daughter late returning
From the winter ball

This morning's grains are born in sterile labs
To some a crime against the harvest
To others, feeding the multitude
& wasn't Frankenstein a kind of Christ?

We are told by officious narcissi
The final circus has left town
No more lions shall be tamed
Children will never believe
In a bear riding a bicycle
Let alone give praise
To the Corn Pop Queen

& you who know your folk
Peer deeply into time's lens
See a child, holy fool
Laughing in delight
Holding in his smooth palm
A wild seed & in its form
Grasp eternity & know
That his spirit is iron
& his gods endure

(First appeared in We've Seen the Same Horizon, 2019)

Through the Bounty

Sent up the hill to pick currants
From their short bush
Outside the barn
Wood worn silver

She-goat pokes head
Above the Dutch door
In their warren
Red-eyed white rabbits

Will be skinned out of
Their pelts into pots
Of stewed tomatoes

Tomatoes still filling
Bushel baskets
Late in the season

In the coop I shoo hens
Search out brown eggs
Nestled in the straw

Reaching the hill's bottom
Laden with baskets full
A weasel darts past

I race the weasel back up the hill
Those chickens don't work for him

Chapter 4

To Staunch the Blood
After a Fall
from a Great Height
in a Dream

535/4

The rock in my hand
Millions of
Years old but so what

Child Labor

In Memory of Emma Dewhurst Lenz

A broken thread to be rejoined
Young Emma scales the machinery
To reach the bobbins high
Breathing in gulps of cotton dust
Fingers & toes pinched

She will not let them see her cry
She has seen the doffers maimed
Tiny hands smashed
Under the spinning wheels

Snuck out the way they came
Hidden from the law
In smelly wooden crates
On the back of horse carts
Instructed by the minders to lie
Say they slipped under a passing carriage

They will never see her cry
This is Emma's England
Not Edward's
His Majesty, soon dead

Public Morals

She feels herself falling apart
Memories travel to the surface
Splinters
Digs them out with needles
    Making it worse
        She feels herself falling

Fishing in a river of spit
Wishing she had one more hit
Impromptu motel evaporates
    In flashlight beam

She is
Death-frozen lizard deconstructed
By black speck insects
Waterbug on sleeping face
Smashed upon waking
Baby sparrow falling
    From windblown nest
        Decomposing on fresh-cut lawn
        Never singing for worms

My, aren't we quick to judge
Still haven't solved the riddle
        Under our own cap

The Sinner & The Preacher

A wooden church
Stands in the cove
Over distant hills
Clouds cast their shadows
Yet none are clean
In His sight & none
Will escape His wrath

He only touched her
When he struck her
She wore her hair down
To hide the marks
Though no stripes can evade
The glare of God's light

Their cabin down
By the shoals
Was a far piece
Up the road
No Bible did the
Preacher carry there

He knew it was
God's will
When he saw the preacher
At his door
He knew
It was God's will

He beat her
Couldn't keep her
Drove her to the arms
Of the preacher
The hands that prayed with her
Now held aloft a razor

A final act of love
There is healing
In the blood
He offered up his neck
To the man no one'd suspect

The sins he tried to hide
Were written on the outside
By righteous hand & honed steel
They knew it was God's will

Real Estate

Agent Longstroke slithers
In gold sports-coat
Piloting his whip down
Roosevelt & Buchanan
Pointing out the conveniences
To sweet Miss Jones

"Liquor store across from pawn shop
Plenty of dark alleys
For quick, anonymous action"

Miss Jones squirms in the
Sweaty, fuzzy seat
Fingering mauve tube-top
& a puss-filled sore
On her inner-arm

"Endless rows of bodegas & barbershops
Failed Romeo family men
Money deep in their scabrous pockets
Priced to sell"

Loneliness & burning mouth
Hidden with twist of lipstick

"Of course, we'll need to check your credit"

Miss Jones' head drops under dash

Leaning against Japanese car
Daisy studies the fresh-girl

"They sure get familiar around here in a hurry"

Wiping chin with bloody knuckles
(Defensive wounds)

"I'll take it"

Golden arm extends out window
Glock in gold-ringed hand

Daisy drops to the pavement
Cursing her assassin

"To think I built this stroll
When that bitch was in Huggies"

Put up the sold sign

"You'll be very happy here"

Airport

In the hotel
I had a view
Of the airport
   & you

Struggling under
The bartender's spell
Control tower lights
Reflecting
   In your eyes

Little black dress
   Teased hair
Champagne cup breasts
   DC-10 landing gear

Chanel No. 5
   Cutaneous folds
Passion to fly
   Desire
      To crash

In the hotel
I had a view
Of the airport
   & you

First appeared as lyrics on Anger & English
(4 band compilation EP), Framework Records, 1993

Hidden Panel

Under the back stairs
Of a manse
Long abandoned
A hidden room
Sealed up forty years
Judging by the 1950's beefcake photos
Torn from "fitness" magazines
Affixed to the fake wood paneling
Scotch tape yellowed
& cracked

On the floor
A mattress discolored
& bare
Behind it a clothes rack
Full of costumes
Indian maiden, Cleopatra
Harem girl

The old man played
Dress up games?
Not a crime

What was discovered upstairs
In his sister's room
Behind Harlequin Romance
Stuffed Shelves
Rotting in an army duffle
That was a different matter

Soulless Heavens

It's another night
& he's gotten tight
  Nothing is right with the world
  He screams

Hates his god damn job
He's too good for them
(Late once more
& he's out on his ass)

His shouting upsets the children
Mom yells
  Take it outside
   You fat Mick bastard

She's thinking she won't be
Seeing him much more
  & somehow
  She's alright with that

How it gets these days
Takes her back a ways
When her old man
Got loaded each night

Into a rage & another drunk tirade
Mother pretended
  Everything was
  Just fine

Mom escaped into her rosary
"Though prayers never seem
    To work for me"

She's hoping we won't be
Seeing him any more
    & somehow
    Be alright

Raido in Reverse

Over trash clogged ditch
Heron's shadow flits

Soda bottle filled with urine
Label sun-faded

Raccoon carcass drying
On median wall

Herons have all left their nests
High above the swamp

In trees dead yet durable
Totem poles carved by decay

Road fallen onions
Most now smashed

Under traffic-snarled tires
Pavement, onions & raccoon bones

A heron's shadow
Crossing trash filled ditch

Things never glimpsed
Living at full speed

Stronghold

I shall trace my life
Upon this tower
Rising to trespass Heaven's
Indigo rimmed perimeter

Leaden shadows bleed
Upon the tower's face
Descending to its base
While high on parapets
An archer surveils
Enchanted arrows
In endless store

An archer who asks
"Will I now lay down my bow
Even as beast & brute
Come with roar & drum?"

Would you have him pause
Midst onslaught
Pen & knife
Hovering above parchment
Waiting on a ray from above
To pierce his dark
That inspired word might
Contain this flash
Of cathartic light?

May his retiring canto

Brightly sing for you &
Illuminate your halls
Until dearest day
Come again

Chapter 5

An Effective Charm to Remove Glum-Worm from Convent Schools, Ships upon Open Waters, & All Solitary Places of Contemplation

535/5

The moth I'm trying
To kill has
Landed on my leg

Conversion

Attending to the last lepers
In this first colony
Oftentimes think back on
School days & those
Selfless nuns I daily troubled
My well of pranks
Bottomless

      Religieuse du
      Sacré-Cœur de Jésus

Same order who reported
To Pope Paul VI
Sighting of luminous
El-Zeitoun
In broken & defeated
Egypt land

Where (it's been said)
On instruction of Gabriel
Destroyer of bastards & reprobates
The Holy Family fled
Until old Herod croaked

Skip ahead 1,969 years
Take or give
Right before I was last born
Seven Coptic children
Among 15

Rushing to glimpse spectral "Mary"
Crush-killed in the mob's gyre

Our school being converted
Along with convent & chapel
Into luxury condos
Original parquet floors
View of the world's
Tallest grain elevator
Stony Agnes
Lilies & lamb
Removed from storied premises
Her fellow saints & martyrs
Left in unpainted silhouette
Against walls of each barren ambry

Roman house converted
To Roman church
    & back again

Raiders hauled off that heavy
Baptistery in which we plunged
Dirty fingers
To make clean our naughty souls
With wet crosses traced
On smooth brows

Both lectern & pulpit vanished
Along with life sized dying Christ
Chancel & nave
No longer divided

Much space with ripped out pews

    Here sat a Huxley
    & there a Trudeau
    The rest of them names
    You wouldn't know

Laity & liturgy
Have left the building

High over the Hudson
The Sacred Heart Sisters'
Mortal remains remain
Black iron crosses
Uniform rows
Rigid behind locked gate
Bordering our soccer field
Where the Blue & Green
Played the Farm
    Reform school kids
Age 20 in 10th grade
Guarded by coaches
Shouldering shotguns
    Full of rock salt

The track circling its perimeter
Not quite a true quarter mile
Don't get too excited
By your time

Operation Wreck You

Shower us with splinters
      Crucifix rain
Our centers liquefy
What is made will be unmade
Direct us, kind Virgil
Past she-wolf & greyhound
Alley bat & lecherous professor

Taint us, paint us
Give in to mutilations
Beasts & their marksmen

You have been robbed
Of a thousand Xmas memories
Of purity & appetite
      Danger & vision

You have been robbed
      Of adventure
Everything is an emergency

Godmonster

Through a labyrinth of
Xmas trees spitting dead needles
Onto rat fur carpet
You see my papier-mâché
Bull mask
& laugh

& all the bulbs
That failed to light
Are wrapped around
My hand too tight
Not so much a man
I am a process that repeats
Not a milking cow
(You know that much now)

Some find me
An ornament, fragile yet enduring
Among the burning branches
Or under hot rocks fallen
From ancient skies

You have yet to discover
Whether I am a builder of nests
For songbirds
Or scorpions

(First appeared in An Anthology of Poems from The Red Salon, 2018)

Saint Agnes School

The nuns serve brioche
Bursting with choking hazards
Diminutive racecars
Jax & coins
Baked in each slice
Tiny pink plastic baby-doll
Found by some kid
Who isn't me & I don't like
Extending to this jerk
Certain rights & privileges
Signified by the paper crown
Set upon his brow

Spit brown penny into my palm
Minted in the year I was born
This, plus 19 more
Will buy a Harvey Comic
At Coulson's News

Close of Lenten season
Stop pretending
I've given up my bad habit
Twisting locks of hair out of my head
To watch them fall from the top bunk
To the toy strewn floor

We kinder cut loose
Into the crabgrass & clover
Beyond the rain corroded slide & swings

Muddy blue Keds
Stomp benign honeybees
Mistaken for bastard yellowjackets

Do you like butter?
We ask our friends
Petite yellow buds under their chins
Dandelion mamas have babies
Heads pop off to mischievous sniggering

Our mission
To hunt down some Easter trophy
A nun directs us towards a
Hedgerow where I am first to discover
The glazed ceramic, halleluiah egg

I am saddened to find it empty

Death Wish as a Prequel to Cinderella

In the back of the VW station wagon
Sweating under an unseasonable wool blanket
Pulled tight over our sunburned faces
"Get down! Stay quiet!"
Father shouts from behind the wheel
We roll to a stop
A guard saunters out of her shack

Father insists that there are no other passengers
Besides mother & himself
I can hear suspicion in the guard's voice
A flashlight beam dances over our hiding place

Miraculously we are waved through
After father buys only two tickets
For a double feature of Cinderella
      & Deathwish

Two films tangentially about
The foolish lengths that parents will go
For the ones they love

Was she truly wicked, this stepmother?
Left alone to care for unlovable daughters
Who would always be clumsy, lumpy
      & ugly
No matter how many buttons & bows
She sewed on their ballgowns
Love, it has been said

Is doing whatever is necessary

& so, she hid away their rival
For the affections & fortunes
Of the King's only heir

Hid her away under mask of ash
Isolated in her attic room
This pretty girl went insane
Talking to mice & taking their side
Against the cat whose only wish
Was to rid their home of these diseased vermin

The second film begun, & father shouted
"Go to sleep!"
We came to the drive-in dressed in pajamas
The fire-retardant chemicals in the fabric
Seeping into our bloodstream
Doing god knows what damage to our DNA

I did try to obey
Screams from the speaker junction box
Rattled me out of light slumber
Peeking over the seat I saw bandits
Tearing open Cinderella's blouse
Later, she was sectioned to the asylum
Unable to speak

Perhaps the first film, a cartoon
Was her dream while committed

Her maddened father took to the streets
A pouncing cat
& I see that the 17th Century kingdom
Was all along
Our grimy, barbarian 1970s New York

With his daughter locked away
In a tower
Alone with her racing thoughts
Her tongue still
She cannot stop her father from
Exterminating the vermin

There are no good mice
In a plague year

Destroying the Animal

Braced against electric fence
Legs sheared off above all four knees
Blood trail from road
Staining the thin coating of snow

Below us a farm
Not cold enough to freeze the pond
      Aim & take my shot
Bleating collapses

Driver thanks me
We examine damage
To front quarter panel
Of white Sprinter van

His expression - disbelief & terror
Eyes drawn to spot to which our
Deer dragged herself
Agonized locomotion on exposed bone

She just wanted to live
      Don't we all?
It's impossible for her
My pity turns to fury
      Why are you making me
           Kill you again?

Carotid artery
Flashes panicked SOS

Answer with bullets

Resonance booming
    Across the hills

Oftentimes a truck will stop
Man will ask can he take that deer
To be processed & stored
In his deep freezer

Even the most mangled bucks
Have antlers or whole head
Sawed off for trophies
Headless bodies left behind
    For buzzards

Not our doe, all but
Eviscerated
On impact

First appeared in The Asylum Diaries: Autopsy!
* (Oscillate Wildly Press, 2019)*

Charmless

Masks & egos binned
In Gehenna yesterdays
Diamondback skin shed
Still you stalk at the garden gate
      Ready to behead
With the sharp end of a hoe

Did my bane reach your heart?

I am not as you imagine
Coiled under rotting leaves
Dead shrew in my fangs
Malevolence in my moving heart

Your senses vainly search
The low places
I am no longer among the things
That crawleth

Body burned away
Sentience eclipsed by fatidic shadow
& yet my evidence
Cannot be destroyed

In the end too
There will be
The Word
& my Word
Is venom

Chapter 6

A Talisman to Protect
Against Elf-Shot, Witch-Stab,
& All Paranormal Attack

535/6

Know this: I deal with
The topside
World at my leisure

Bolt Failure

The Lieutenant: What plea do you enter to the charge of treason, most egregious?

Frau Sonnen: Guilty! There can be no doubt! Prepared I am to meet my deserved fate & a greater judgement that awaits me in eternity!

The Tragedy of the Sunmaid, Act II, Scene 3

+++

He read aloud these lines from his play
Written in tight cursive
In secret spiral
Notebook

Unable to command
Her heart
He attempted to master
A library of knots
This would be his undoing

Thirteen turns made thirteen coils
Should have stopped at eight
Stickler for tradition
Greased rope with tallow

Smooth bolt
Passed through uppermost coils

Confident this would prevent
Rope from cinching down
Far enough to constrict
Vessels in his neck

For this dress rehearsal
In which he played
Her role
Her underpants served as
Blindfold & mask

Knot behind his left ear
Stepping off the folding chair
To entropy and beyond
Feet convulsing inches above
Basement floor littered with
Sinister pencil roughs
Of their little daughter
Tied supine
To the coffee table

As it often does
In calamities resulting
From poor engineering
It all came down to one bolt

Oiled rope now bearing
His portly frame
Spit out steel pin
Hollow refrain as it bounced
Across cement

Wicked pleasure
In meticulous planning
He attributed to the idiom
"The devil is in the details"
The origin & meaning of which
He truly failed to grasp

Long after his naked body
Ceased running in place
Kicking & twitching
Unwitting actress
For whom this role was written
Returned home
Cut him down from the beam
In disgust and shame
Snatched her panty
From his surprised face
Hid those hideous sketches
Had a smoke
& called it in

They never found that bolt
Which bounced behind
The old Maytag
Coming to rest
In a nest of nails, tacks & lint

Community Corrections

Dead in a ditch
Throat slit
Tricked out bicycle
Thrown on top
Bloodless corpse

Boy was warned but
Can't tell some vatos nothing
& *these people*
Only warn *once*

File closed "by death"
In less time than it took me
To brew our first pot
Of bad coffee

God Is Very Angry

God is very angry with you sister
One of these days
He's going to lay you low

You turned away a love
That would not leave you
Laid down with the one
Who would deceive you
Promised you the easy life
Now you're sucking off death
Through a glass pipe

God is very angry with you
Oh, my sister
One of these days
He'll lay you low

God's been very angry
Brother, my brother
The time is come
He'll lay you low

You blew into town
With your guitar
Sold your shiny soul
To be a star
Now your strings are gone
& you're strung out
There's a pimp on the corner

Gonna turn you out

God is very angry with you sinners
The hour must come
He's bound to lay you low

She Built a Bomb

This night is solid
Or made of specks
Either way it shakes
Creosote excitements
Won't let you sleep

Your university taught you
Better violence through physics
Your mind is a casket
Full of math that turns to ash
Quantum abstractions
That burn this world to ash

They taught you how to keep
      Secrets
Swallow hard
      Pretend to forget
To live submerged
Without breathing

Your dying geranium
Could have shown you
How to let in the light
Like you she's stuck inside
As a darkness built of dust
Encloses you
& your trembling hands

Hands that shake

In front of your face
Holding a cigarette
You struggle to light

Abomination mother
Summoner of the poison wind
Cowards & heroes
Are equal in your sight

You always had a head for numbers

In through the mail slot
A sliver of accusing sunshine
Accompanies final notices
Dropping to an entryway
Carpeted with months of
Unopened envelopes
Ad circulars
Unread newspapers

In the bed you never leave
Sour milk sheets
Send barbed wire strokes
Against your broke-down backside
Pickle jars brimful of reddish piss
Crowd a nightstand charred
By stubbed out smokes
Hot ash from your Salem Slim
Falls to the floor
You exhale smoke
As a broadside morass ignites

After years of hiding
You step into the light

Unwanted Apparatus

This emergency set up
Is a damned
Nuisance

It calls people
Even when I don't
Need help

It is waking neighbors
I want you to stop it
Immediately

I am disconnecting
These wires

You must get
This fool machinery
& take it away

Chapter 7

To Protect Parchment from Burns or Tears (Said to Be Infallible)

535/7

Bike messenger girl
Please take heart
Heaven sings our names

Blood Castles

Three wise men went out walking
Coming to the edge of a nameless sea
Full moon and clement sun shared the pale sky
Each man drew his blade
Casting them into the arcane water

The man from the east sighed as his knife
Sunk into the coral
The man from the west groaned as his knife
Floated beyond the horizon

The man who was from neither north nor south
Waited for the moon to stir the water &
Carry his knife back to shore

He cut the throat of the man from the east
He slashed the wrists of the man from the west

Tasting his tears, he turned the blade &
Plunged it into his own heart
As he bled out upon the white sand
A city appeared across the water
He dreamt a new home for his children
To be protected forevermore

But we are not so safe

FROM MY DREAM DIARY:

BOARD THE OPEN-AIR SKY TRAIN that follows the elf-hidden tracks of the Wild Hunt. We ascended into pallid winter heavens, bound north to a Yukon of the soul. Below, a de-evolved cave dweller crossing a bridge of ladders bound together with bungee cords and duct tape. Fallout from future wars burned away all vegetation. He will eat cold beets from a can over which he clubbed another man to death.

We make good mythic-time. Arriving at our first station, as a baroque darkness cascades from a sky of black starflowers. I stand on the shore of a lake from which rise phosphorous sapphire clouds. Spectral, starry towers, lost to our world, have reappeared in this place. They are bathed in pale azure light of two thousand ghosts.

An unlike-sun rises. We rumble high above palm trees and beach huts, further north than they have any right to be. All around I see dazzling colors outside our possible spectrum, beyond the palate of earthly eyes. In seas immaculate, sacrificial fish offer themselves up to shark gods. Mother shark sees me above. She admonishes me not to judge the cull. Her lineage is far older than mine, she says, and has achieved a perfection surpassing our wisdom, faith and reason.

Dinner bell! The stevedore has hauled up

our dinner in nets from stoic waters. Frozen tentacles of some ancient cephalopod are passed around. We gnaw sea salty meat with primitive teeth.

We are underway to that kind of Yukon existing between the natural and the fabulous, a region beyond death's illusory borders. Yet I remember:

…her legs over mine in a crowded café. Leaving for home before the coffee is served. Encircling her tiny waist with hot breath kisses.

I open my eyes, returning to my love and her universe.

BROKE INTO A CHANGE MACHINE at a public park. Kali Ma stands lookout. She has put me up to this theft. "You need those coins to feed the machines at the laundromat." I carry them in cupped hands to a getaway car, left running. "Take the half you are entitled to and leave the rest for another in need."

I detect a security camera aimed at me. "The eye of Shiva!" she yells. I protest "You told me to steal!" and she answers, "Salvation is not free. You thought you had no choice but to steal. Shiva sees all and has no choice but to punish."

I must change my appearance. Shave off my beard in the marble bathroom of a mastersuite in which my mother sleeps. She calls out "It is still late at night. Not yet time for you to wake."

A FAMILY OF CABARET SINGERS is touring a lakeside college with their son. Walking back to their van on the top of a parking deck, they see three dark haired, fat men stripped naked, face down and quite dead on plastic sheets. A gang of killers, clad in shiny black leather, closes in on them. The leader is an older balding and bearded man He is flanked by a young swarthy fellow with a pointy goatee, and an even younger lithe, dark skinned girl. They are wearing matching dangling earrings. The leader tells the family they have just killed the fat men, who were Russian scientists, for their astrophysics secrets…and they are next.

Before the gang can eliminate the witnesses the family leap from the parking deck into the lake below. In addition to being professional singers, it turns out they are expert swimmers, and make sport of the mile long distance to the other side of the lake. They exit the lake, breathless and spy a luxury hotel on the hill above. Dripping wet, they sneak in through an open window into a guest suite. Their son, who always looks on the bright side, smiles and makes the comment that jumping into the lake, was the first time he was warm all day - as the water was quite comfortable.

On exiting the room they mistake a waiter delivering room service for one of the killers. Dad breaks the hapless gent's arm by pinning him to the hallway wall with the door.

The scene changes to one week later - the waiter's arm is in a sling. He gives a friendly wave to the dad of the family who gently pats him on the shoulder. Father and son are now working as cabaret singers at the hotel restaurant and are sharply dressed in black tuxedos.

Mom was not hired as the hotel already had a female singer. Father and son are both enthralled by this woman, who is formally attired in a widow's black costume. She is Spanish, in her seventies, and sings passionately with exaggerated, sweeping gestures. They tell mom how much they admire this talented singer, oblivious to mom's anger at not getting hired. Mom makes a crack about the older woman's heavy stage makeup.

Nobody spots the gang of killers, now sitting in the audience.

A YOUNG CLERK at a small town police department has altered all incident reports to be about clowns "even when it wasn't appropriate." It was unclear if she were attempting to smear the town's sizable clown population, whether it was a prank, or due to some behavioral quirk.

RETURNING HOME after the age of man has passed. The overpass is overtaken by cascades of bright hibiscus never seen this far north. They crowd out the native snapdragons that once delighted me as a child. From hillside perch a Holiday Inn, sideways slid looks so small amid the spray of giant flowers. It clings to cliffside, an insignificant ornament out of time in this hanging garden. The outdoor pool now swallowed by vines.

Follow the exit down to a stand of kingly oak trees whose circumference tells me that I have arrived here hundreds of years from the days I last wore flesh. Sunlight through the branches forms three prismatic, compass-point stars. I can travel this road no further and stand barefoot in pungent mud. I seem to have lost my shoes some time ago.

The brown river has flooded the banks and washed over the pavement. In a world without men, there is no need for my father's wandering guise. Shall I instead be a wise gardener?

Samsara

Let the children have cupcakes
& furniture to jump on
Ten more minutes before bedtime

You know what's coming
Let them have some joy before

For all we know
Five or six years before tonight
Their souls were leaving broken bodies
In a Mexico City traffic accident
Awaiting divine judgement in a Serbian nursing home
Or floating above their wasted carcass
Remorseful at having reached the end
On a bare mattress in some Berlin squat

If we are all still here
In this final age of iron
None of us have ascended
We might just be the dumbest of the dumb
If that's the way it works

Give them an extra brownie
& a hug
You'll need it more than them

(Will first appear in The Scriblerus, Fall 2019)

Drawing by Alec K. Redfearn

Jason O'Toole is the author of *Spear of Stars* and has also been featured in *An Anthology of Poems from The Red Salon* and *We've Seen the Same Horizon*, all from The Red Salon. He was the original vocalist for the NY Hardcore Punk band, Life's Blood. These days, he collaborates with composer-musicians Alec K. Redfearn & Herr Lounge Corps, in multiple clandestine and possibly dangerous schemes that are not necessarily for public consumption.